Editor-in-Chief and Founder:
  Lyndon H. LaRouche, Jr.
Editorial Board: *Lyndon H. LaRouche, Jr. , Helga
  Zepp-LaRouche, Robert Ingraham, Tony
  Papert, Gerald Rose, Dennis Small, Jeffrey
  Steinberg, William Wertz*
Co-Editors: *Robert Ingraham, Tony Papert*
Managing Editor: *Nancy Spannaus*
Technology: *Marsha Freeman*
Books: *Katherine Notley*
Ebooks: *Richard Burden*
Graphics: *Alan Yue*
Photos: *Stuart Lewis*
Circulation Manager: *Stanley Ezrol*

INTELLIGENCE DIRECTORS
Counterintelligence: *Jeffrey Steinberg, Michele
  Steinberg*
Economics: *John Hoefle, Marcia Merry Baker,
  Paul Gallagher*
History: *Anton Chaitkin*
Ibero-America: *Dennis Small*
Russia and Eastern Europe: *Rachel Douglas*
United States: *Debra Freeman*

INTERNATIONAL BUREAUS
Bogotá: *Miriam Redondo*
Berlin: *Rainer Apel*
Copenhagen: *Tom Gillesberg*
Houston: *Harley Schlanger*
Lima: *Sara Madueño*
Melbourne: *Robert Barwick*
Mexico City: *Gerardo Castilleja Chávez*
New Delhi: *Ramtanu Maitra*
Paris: *Christine Bierre*
Stockholm: *Ulf Sandmark*
United Nations, N.Y.C.: *Leni Rubinstein*
Washington, D.C.: *William Jones*
Wiesbaden: *Göran Haglund*

ON THE WEB
e-mail: eirns@larouchepub.com
www.larouchepub.com
www.executiveintelligencereview.com
www.larouchepub.com/eiw
Webmaster: *John Sigerson*
Assistant Webmaster: *George Hollis*
Editor, Arabic-language edition: *Hussein Askary*

EIR (ISSN 0273-6314) *is published weekly
(50 issues), by EIR News Service, Inc.,
P.O. Box 17390, Washington, D.C. 20041-0390.
(703) 777-9451 ext. 415*

European Headquarters: E.I.R. GmbH, Postfach
Bahnstrasse 9a, D-65205, Wiesbaden, Germany
Tel: 49-611-73650
Homepage: http://www.eirna.com
e-mail: eirna@eirna.com
Director: Georg Neudecker

Montreal, Canada: 514-461-1557

Denmark: EIR - Danmark, Sankt Knuds Vej 11,
basement left, DK-1903 Frederiksberg, Denmark.
Tel.: +45 35 43 60 40, Fax: +45 35 43 87 57. e-mail:
eirdk@hotmail.com.

Mexico City: EIR, Sor Juana Inés de la Cruz 242-2
Col. Agricultura C.P. 11360
Delegación M. Hidalgo, México D.F.
Tel. (5525) 5318-2301
eirmexico@gmail.com

Canada Post Publication Sales Agreement
#40683579

Postmaster: Send all address changes to *EIR*, P.O.
Box 17390, Washington, D.C. 20041-0390.

Signed articles in *EIR* represent the views of the
authors, and not necessarily those of the Editorial
Board.

As London Launches Operation Chaos

EDITORIAL

Agents of History

Oct. 7—On December 1, 1998, José López Portillo, the former President of the Republic of Mexico, declaimed, "It is now necessary for the world to listen to the wise words of Lyndon LaRouche."

That warning, that admonition, carries more pungency and more urgency today than on the day that it was uttered.

As events unfold, with warnings of an impending financial crash coming from many different sides and numerous individuals, it is of utmost importance that all of us listen to the "wise words" of Lyndon LaRouche. In truth, none of the transAtlantic players on the field, even among the more insightful, have put forward proposals that indicate that they know what it is that must be done. Their minds are operating within layers of nested boxes, and their solutions are, at best, piecemeal; at worst, they are ludicrous.

Our mission is to represent the highest standard and to fight—from the standpoint of history and as allies and friends of Lyndon LaRouche— for LaRouche's policy. We should

EIRNS/Stuart Lewis
Statue of Alexander Hamilton in front of the U.S. Treasury Building.

advocate and battle for nothing less.

In a discussion with the LPAC Policy Committee and others on October 7, LaRouche said this:

All you have to do is to take my laws, which I presented. Those laws, my laws, define exactly what solves the problem by creating a standard by which credit is defined. This was developed by the Treasurer of the United States [Alexander Hamilton]. This is the only way it will work ...

My national laws—those were whose laws? Not mine. I was the one who set up the standard for that, and they didn't do much about it. Therefore, all you have to do is go for an international program based on that principle, the same principle, and you've got to get the people of the nations working together to understand what this kind of action is. Just read the publications on law by [Hamilton]. He wrote the laws. They're written there. But people don't do it. They talk about something else. Therefore, they don't understand what makes history, what makes history work. What I did was actually a mechanism to define the way in which the original system had been established. By Hamilton. You don't have to do anything else. That's what you have to do . . .

You're talking about Hamilton's laws, and you're talking about my laws. That's what you're talking about. Don't change the subject . . . You have to get an international agreement among nations, among a significant number of nations, which will create a credit system, an international credit system or something tantamount to that, which will deal with this problem. We're not talking about that, yet. You have to talk about that; you've got to talk about the work of Hamilton. You've got to put the name of Hamilton in there, and you've got to put my name in there. Because that's the only way you're going to get that thing done.

Get some books about Hamilton's economy. It's all there. All I did was to put this thing into standards which conform to what Hamilton laid out. People have to take the handbooks, the records of Hamilton; read those things as Hamilton stipulates. Use that. Do it! Then you can go to the table and say, 'Now we can create a credit system.' Take Hamilton, and take what I have done. Put the two things together, and that work contains enough information to define exactly what has to be done. It's just ignored because people want to be stupid.

The danger in merely quoting from LaRouche is that what is presented is a one-sided argument in which LaRouche says "the following," and, oftentimes, members respond by saying, "LaRouche says this, but I am going to do something else, because I know better." Something more practical, more limited. And that sets a different agenda.

The quotations here from LaRouche are not "his" policy. They must be the policy orientation of all of us in the LaRouche movement—LPAC, *EIR*, the Manhattan Project, and every member. We represent the leadership, under LaRouche's direction, in this crisis. What we say, what we do is critical, and we must act accordingly. We are agents of history, not practical politicians.

EIR Contents

www.larouchepub.com Volume 43, Number 42, October 14, 2016

Cover This Week

Prince Charles (foreground) takes part in sword dance in Saudi Arabia, 2014.

youtube Royal Family Channel

READ ALEXANDER HAMILTON!

The Science of Victory

by Dennis Speed

Oct. 12—The LaRouche Manhattan Project, which has been circulating the broadsheet called *The Hamiltonian* for the past ten weeks, is now deployed to organize the "American organization"—the citizenry—to galvanize the Congress into reinstating the Glass Steagall Act. That, however, could never be done by appealing to the Congress to act as such. As with the September 28 victory against Obama's override of the Justice Against Sponsors of Terrorism Act (JASTA), a "Classical musical principle" must be introduced. This must be done by reintroducing the people of New York City to the real Alexander Hamilton.

Hamilton has, unfortunately, been getting the wrong kind of attention lately as a result of the eponymous Broadway musical. Reading Hamilton and comparing his work with Lyndon LaRouche's Four Laws (see p. 11) would, however, give the citizens of Manhattan a chance to repay the debt they owe him for founding their city, and the United States Presidency, by summarily defeating the Wall Street-based treason that assassinated him in 1804. Since the writing of Alexander Hamilton's four great reports—on manufactures, on credit, on the national bank, and on the constitutionality of a national bank—there has been an established Presidential practice, in the form of the Washington/ Hamilton Administration, that is the standard for the functioning of the Executive

LPAC/Sylvia Rosas

A musical principle is required to return the United States to a Hamiltonian Presidency.

branch of government in any republic, and not only for the United States.

This standard has rarely been replicated in the American Presidency itself. For example, neither the Adams, nor the Jefferson, nor the Madison, nor the Monroe Presidency was of the caliber of that first Presidential administration. The one term of John Quincy Adams (and the notable service of Quincy Adams in the Congress subsequently) and the one term of Abraham Lincoln, met that standard. All Presidents other than these three, between 1790 and 1865, were failures when it came to the matter of the principle of the Presidency so established in Hamilton's reports. Some, like Andrew Jackson, Martin Van Buren, and James Buchanan, were direct opponents of it.

Why Slavery Continues Today

Largely because of the failure to implement Hamilton's reports, there was only a partially successful battle fought in the United States to end slavery, including in 1865. Those earlier failures were to cripple and limit the well-intentioned and partially successful Grant Administration, which was more successful than had been admitted until only recently by historians no longer devoted to "Confederate" interpretations of the 1861-65 conflict. The continuing legacy of British imperial financial control over the lives of Americans and others worldwide, is what has actually defined the failures of the American Presidency since the time before the Revolution, since the British East India Company was in reality never eradicated. Hamilton's measures have rarely even been invoked by Presidents, much less attempted.

In one sense, Hamilton's four reports were all aimed at freeing every man and woman from slavery to the British Crown. "Slavery" should refer here not merely to the obvious African slave trade and its accompanying atrocities, the which affected tens of millions.

Slavery, albeit in different forms, exists today, precisely because the deeper principle contained in Hamilton's work goes unappreciated. What about the slavery of mass drug abuse throughout today's United States, including the "white suburbia" heroin epidemic? What about the debt-slavery that is the present circumstance of most of the globe in the form of the dead trans-Atlantic monetary system and its various "country agents"? Look at the state of literacy in today's America, and remember that literacy on the part of the slave, if discovered, was punishable by death. The first step up from slavery was literacy. What is therefore, from that standpoint, the true condition of the "non-cursive reading" youth population of the United States today?

American Revolutionary economic policy derived from the battle against the wage slavery, debt slavery, and chattel slavery of the British Crown (see box). It derived from the active organization by Washington's military aides—Hamilton, John Laurens, and Lafayette—along with Hamilton's close friends, New Yorkers Gouverneur Morris and the spymaster John Jay, of a movement to end slavery in the United States. (By the way, could they have carried that out without the tacit approval of their commander?)

They failed in that effort to end chattel slavery in the short term. It was, however, Hamilton's four documents—adopted by Washington—that proposed the means to force the elimination of all forms of British imperial monetary coercion, including chattel slavery, by the creation of a national form of credit, banking,

The British Maintained Slavery In the American Colonies

The following is an excerpt from Journal of a Voyage to the United States *by Auguste Levasseur, private secretary to the Marquis de Lafayette during his 1824-1825 visit to the United States. It demonstrates that Virginia was prevented, by Britain, from abolishing the slave trade 80 years before the 1861-65 War of the Secession, and that it was recognized by that time that slavery was in fact a counter-productive system that ensured the deeper physical and moral impoverishment of the United States in the southern region of the nation.*

This crime, by which a man, misusing his strength and his understanding, subjects to his whims or to the satisfaction of his needs, another man less educated than he, and reduces him to the condition of slavery, was perpetrated in Virginia in 1620. It had as perpetrators the misery of the Colonists whose wearied and ill-fed bodies could no longer make the soil productive, and the avarice of the Dutch who delivered to them, like beasts of burden, some unfortunate Negroes whom they had stolen in the sands of Africa in order to sell them later. The English, no less eager for silver than the Dutch, soon turned to this abuse of power, which fosters idleness, as a source of wealth, and they hastened to exploit it to their profit, and from that time their vessels poured out thousands of Slaves annually on the American continent. Nonetheless the sentiments of humanity that famine had for some time stifled in the hearts of the Virginian Colonists revived with the return of fortune and plenty.

In about the year 1680, the General Assembly of the State of Virginia requested of the parent state that it finally put an end to this commerce in human flesh, infamous and unnecessary in the future, since now the population was numerous enough and active enough to cultivate a land that required only the lightest work to reward the tiller richly. Other Colonies repeated this cry of justice and philanthropy, but the parent country was callous and responded only by this atrocious resolution of Parliament: *The importation of Slaves in America is too lucrative for the Colonies to be able to insist that England renounce it forever.* This response was accompanied by threats to which it was necessary to succumb since they were in no condition to resist them. Nonetheless, the General Assembly renewed several times its demand. [Emphasis in the original.]

and manufacturing to be deployed through the Presidency of the United States. This was what Franklin Delano Roosevelt—a descendant of the Isaac Roosevelt who cofounded the Bank of New York with Alexander Hamilton—understood as the function of the Presidency. Roosevelt's "New Deal" was actually a return to the "old deal" that Hamilton's documents had established with the help of FDR's ancestor.

Roosevelt's "New Deal" was actually a return to the "old deal" that Hamilton's documents had established with the help of FDR's ancestor. On the left, Alexander Hamilton; on the right, Franklin D. Roosevelt.

Reinstate Hamilton's System Now!

Incredibly, Barack Obama gave a recent interview purporting to favorably compare his 2009-2016 performance as President with that of Franklin Roosevelt. Please!

The Barack Obama Administration would be, hands down, the worst of Presidential failures in American history, were the Cheney/Bush Administration not to have immediately preceded it. Obama's recent statements and actions regarding the Russian campaign against Washington's and London's ISIS in Syria, along with those coming from the camp of Democratic nominee Hillary Clinton, could also mean that the Obama Presidency may be the last.

Luckily, Vladimir Putin, and the leadership of China, have a considerably greater grasp of the principles of the American Presidency than any of the present or prospective occupants of the White House. That might not be enough to keep us alive, but it is an essential advantage for American citizens, who can be confident that manifestations of the real character of the American Presidential system on their part will be recognized and welcomed as "the real McCoy" by the two most powerful nations in the world outside of the United States. Obama's defeat in the Congress on September 28—in the Congressional override of his veto of JASTA—was greeted with more genuine relief and pleasure in those circles than is now appreciated.

In his address to the Manhattan town meeting on October 1, Lyndon LaRouche commented on the victory that had been won in the Congress through the repudiation of Barack Obama's veto of JASTA:

I think the essential thing is to concentrate on what the Congress did in that landslide … The problem is now, we've got to take what we can do with our own United States; get our own United States population put into order. Use the experience that we reached in that event; use that to remind yourself of what we, the people in the United States, can do of their own will, as they did in that override. And that's it. We can now; we've got to fight some enemies, there's no question about that; that's a fact. And that lesson from the way the Congress voted in that one case, that's your cue to win …

How to Stop the Bankers' Crimes

Later, responding to another question, LaRouche remarked:

Wall Street has lost the war. Now, they haven't declared that; but they have lost the power of money, and it's going to be fully taken away from them in due course. So therefore, that's the way we ought to look at this thing. We are going to take their dollars and so forth away; not to take anything that they own, but to prevent them from wasting our money.

A few days later, in a Friday webcast, LaRouche associate Paul Gallagher filled out how that might be done, in describing how to effectively reinstate the Glass-Steagall Act of 1933 that was rescinded in 1999:

> The way to do that is to enact the Glass-Steagall Act; put it back into effect. Essentially, you make such a fence around the deposits then that the sharks absolutely have no access, and you will find that those speculative units—many of them—will rapidly be bankrupt.
>
> We're very happy to hear a proposal from a legislator in Hamburg in Germany yesterday, to do exactly that with Deutsche Bank. If it can be done with Deutsche Bank, as Lyndon and Helga LaRouche proposed a couple of months ago, then it can be done with any major bank in the world. If you can actually get back a real bank, a commercial bank, a lending bank out of that monstrosity, that mess which is Deutsche Bank today that's in the process of failing, then the only way to do it is with the proposal this legislator made. It is the same proposal that Lyndon and Helga LaRouche had made two months ago, known as the Herrhausen Proposal for Deutsche Bank. That legislator said to separate and in an orderly way, run down, eliminate all of these toxic, speculative units. Then the commercial bank may be capitalized, even by the government, in such a way that it begins to invest seriously in the economy.
>
> So that's what is not being discussed—the crimes and how to stop them. That's a much more fundamental question than which of these banks is going to go first and be the trigger for the general liquidity explosion. We have to get the Congress to return. What are they doing? They leave Washington for two months after saying they want to get tough with Wall Street in a series of hearings on Wells Fargo's crimes . . .

Glass-Steagall's reinstatement would not be an American initiative: It would be a world initiative. It would not be a "banking reform": It would be a political revolution. It would not merely "break up the big banks"; it would create the basis for the issuance of directed national credit for physical economic improvements.

The reinstatement of Glass-Steagall would empower the United States Treasury to issue credit to provide a catalyst not merely to "build new infrastructure," but to create a new world economic platform in conjunction with the BRICS and other nations, designed by La-Rouche and termed the World Land-Bridge, a process already under way in Asia and other parts of the world. It would allow the Presidency to commit the United States to a new Moon mission, joining the Chinese in their quest to investigate the far side of the Moon and mine helium-3 for thermonuclear fusion power—power generated for Earth use and for space flight, specifically for missions to Mars and other planetary bodies. Glass-Steagall's reinstatement would be "Hamiltonian."

Wherein Lies the Power of the Human Being?

This "Hamilton initiative" follows upon the successful "living memorial" campaign carried out by the Manhattan Project one month ago, at the center of which was the participation of its members in the performance and organizing of four concerts comprising African-American Spirituals and Mozart's *Requiem*. Immediately on the heels of those concerts, a stunning defeat was handed to the "untouchable" Barack Obama in both houses of Congress, an unexpected, total repudiation of everything that Obama stands for. In the aftermath of that victory, there has been an attempt to create fear and disgust among the otherwise highly moralized American population, which suddenly realized that it had the capacity to soar above victimization and rout the "foul and pestilent congregation of vapors" daily emanating from the Executive Branch, as well as the Congress itself.

The ugliness that usually prevails in U.S. political life was pierced by Mozart's higher idea of man, and that higher idea did not merely moralize those fighting for a particular victory in the Congress. That higher idea of man is spread in the form of what the physicist Bernhard Riemann termed *Geistesmassen*—"thought-masses," in rough translation. There are ideas that are specific expressions of universal principles, and are therefore not propagated in the normal way that people presume.

They are propagated poetically: As Percy Shelley says in his poem, "Mont Blanc," "The everlasting universe of things flows through the mind." Ideas presented in the guise of poetry, which is composed of the two elements of drama and music, travel far more quickly and reach far more deeply than prose. For example, whether one speaks English, Italian, German, Wolof, Arabic, Chinese, or dialects of any or all of the above, the characteristic of Mozart's *Requiem* is comprehensible to all.

EIRNS/Sylvia Rosas

The September 9-12 performances of the Mozart Requiem in New York and New Jersey radiated a universal principle of human creativity. Here, the Schiller Institute Chorus performing Mozart's Requiem in the Mass at St.Joseph's Co-Cathedral in Brooklyn, New York on Sept. 11, 2016.

The universality of Classical music and culture reaffirms the truth of the oneness of the human race—its creativity. That is the reason that a Congolese airline pilot, with only a modest musical background, can organize his fellow citizens to learn and perform Beethoven's Ninth Symphony, in some cases making their own instruments in order to do so. The Kinshasa Symphony Orchestra made its instruments, not merely because they "practically" had to make them, because they could not get them otherwise; they made the instruments because they had to play the Ninth Symphony.

After decades of senseless wars, all instigated by the Belgian, British, NATO, and Anglo-American conceit of "global imperial dominance," they wished, intended, and succeeded in performing one of the greatest discoveries in the history of humanity, Beethoven's Ninth Symphony. They did this, not only for their own souls' sake, but for the sake of the more than six million that had died in the ongoing wars since 1997. Their humanity did not simply cry out to be recognized; their humanity chose to sing out, instead, and was immediately recognized, because the world was left no choice: Beethoven was speaking from the Congo.

A Sudden, Pungent Convergence

The September 9-12 performances of the Mozart *Requiem* in New York and New Jersey radiated a universal principle of human creativity into a United States disgusted with itself for accepting a crime against its citizens and against humanity—the bombing of the World Trade Center on September 11 and its coverup. Concurrently, a potent, higher view of humanity was also being expressed in the drive to override Barack Obama's opposition to bringing the true killers of September 11 to justice, and that higher idea was being unanimously supported by members of the otherwise moribund, but potentially mobilizable Congress.

The radiating effect of the performances and the drive against the September 11 killers converged, suddenly, in a possibility for action, a blow that could be struck for humanity against the British empire and Obama, its main representative in the United States.

Like an earlier action taken against the infamous New York colonial governor, the "fabulous" Lord Cornbury, "the worst governor ever appointed in the American colonies," the cynosure of the cesspool of degeneracy that was and always shall be the British Crown, the action taken to override Barack Obama's veto was delivered with spice, with "pungency and force." It was a brief glimpse of not only the true character of the American people, but also of the power available through America to humanity as a whole, "to do right." That power affected people that did not hear the performances, did not know that they even happened, and have no idea of what Mozart sounds like.

The Next Irresistible Resonance

Percy Shelley admonishes us that "the mind in creation is as a fading coal, which some invisible influence, like an inconstant wind, awakens to transitory brightness; this power arises from within, like the color of a flower which fades and changes as it is developed, and the conscious portions of our natures are unprophetic either of its approach or its departure."

So something else will have to be done to accomplish this next campaign's objective of implementing the Four Laws of LaRouche and mastering Hamilton's four reports. A new, musical idea is required.

The regular Saturday solfège classes with Diane Sare, designed to teach people to read music and to sing in the context of a fixed "do" system—in which the value of "Middle C" is fixed at 256 cycles per second—is the actual beginning of the LaRouche dialogue. These classes are essential for preparing citizens to creatively act. (As Louis Pasteur once said, "Chance favors only the prepared mind.")

The audience is compelled to "tune up" their minds prior to the discussion. The purpose is to focus the discussion on a singular intent—not a topic, but an idea to be universally grasped. In addition to the classes and weekly choral rehearsals, John Sigerson, director of the music work of the Schiller Institute and leader of the four Mozart performances, is currently lecturing on work pioneered by LaRouche on tuning and registration/voice-placement. The task of every competent orchestra, ensemble, or great performer is to grasp a single musical idea of the composition, to which all other ideas are necessarily subordinate. So it is, also, with organizing the American people to act "in concert."

Sigerson, co-author of the book, *A Manual on Tuning And Registration*, has for nearly 30 years participated in groundbreaking work to returning the nation's and the world's concert stages to what is variously called "scientific tuning," "Verdi pitch," and "proper tuning." For the *Requiem*, Sigerson used his extensive work to tune the voices of the non-professional chorus in such a way as to cause the ensemble to perform and to sound far better than many professional choruses.

It was precisely this choral principle that was used to great effect in the mobilization of the Congress. A unity of effect was created in that body, not merely through "citizen pressure," but through assisting the families of the victims of 9/11, and the courageous few Congressmen that supported them, in their voice-placement. The families and Congressmen were always "saying" the right thing; the problem was to project their message in such a way that an irresistible "shock wave"-like resonance was established that could penetrate even the usually morally opaque Congress.

It worked. And it will be in the higher domain of musical ideas that the campaign to reinstate Glass-Steagall, as a Hamiltonian measure, must find its inspiration to succeed.

FOR ALL MANKIND

What Happened to *Agapē* In Our Exploration of Space?

by Kesha Rogers

We have to build up fast, very fast, the greatest growth of productivity inside nations, now. In other words, we have to understand what mankind is and what mankind must become, fast. We have not yet caught the idea. But we can. So, why don't you start doing it?

—*Lyndon LaRouche*

Oct. 10—What ever happened to the *agapē* in our space program? This very question is fundamental to our continued existence as the *human* species. This is the subject that subsumes Lyndon LaRouche's "Four New Laws" to save immediately the United States, which he introduced in June 2014. What LaRouche presents in this economic platform is not a matter of mere banking policy or of breaking up the big banks. What he prescribes is what is needed to end Wall Street and the financial oligarchy once and for all. What is required is the unleashing of the potential for human creative progress and productivity, a principle embedded in our nation's Declaration of Independence, our Constitution, and its Preamble, and it is expressed in the work of the first Treasury Secretary of our nation, Alexander Hamilton.

LaRouche's four laws are these:

1. The immediate re-enactment of the Glass-Steagall law instituted by U.S. President Franklin D. Roosevelt, without modification, as to principle of action.

2. A return to a system of top-down National Banking, and thoroughly so defined. The precedents for this shall be taken from the banking and credit system established by Alexander Hamilton, as well as Abraham Lincoln's action of creating a national currency ("Greenbacks"), under Presidential authority.

3. The deployment of a new Federal Credit system to generate high-productivity trends in improvements of employment, with the accompanying intention to increase the physical-economic productivity and the standard of living of the persons and households of the United States. An increase in productive employment, as accomplished under Franklin Roosevelt, must reflect an increase in real productivity, coherent with an increase in energy-flux density in the nation's economic practice.

4. The adoption a Fusion-Driver Crash Program. The essential distinction of man from all lower forms of life, and hence, in practice, is that it presents the means for the perfection of the

Wikimedia Commons/Public Domain

LaRouche's four laws rest "on an underlying principle of an unconditional— that is, agapic—love for mankind, to create its future." Here, a portion of The Parable of the Good Samaritan *by Jan Wijnants, 1670, in the State Hermitage Museum, St. Petersburg, Russia.*

specifically affirmative aims and needs of human individual and social life.

Passion Flows from Understanding Man

What is required at this very moment, for this nation and the world, is not merely an economic recovery. We must have a Hamiltonian/LaRouchian vision for an Economic Renaissance. In its essence, it goes far beyond merely building infrastructure and putting people back to work. We must rekindle a passion to create the future! What is required is a complete revolution in science in the terms that LaRouche is demanding today and in what is now being set as a cultural standard in China, as exemplified by the direction of its space program and its commitment to a win-win strategy for mankind.

This revolution in science must start with a renewed conception and understanding of the true nature of mankind—what it means to be truly human. How do we advance the conception of mankind as capable of acting for the benefit of all, from the standpoint that we are thereby going to advance and share in the greatest potentials for mankind that ever existed? This is expressed most poetically in the combination of *1 Corinthians* 13 and in Krafft Ehricke's Three Laws of Astronautics.

That memorable chapter of *1 Corinthians* unfolds the concept of agapic love: "Charity [*agapē*] suffereth long, and is kind; charity envieth not; charity vaunteth not itself, is not puffed up, doth not behave itself unseemly, seeketh not her own, is not easily provoked, thinketh no evil; rejoiceth not in iniquity, but rejoiceth in the truth."

Krafft Ehricke addressed this question of the common aims of mankind in fulfilling its greatest potentials, and saw that the pathway is through "leaving the confines of one small planet" to expand our exploration and settlement to other worlds. To that end, he formulated these Three Laws of Astronautics:

1. Nobody and nothing under the natural laws of this universe [can] impose any limitations on man, except man himself.

2. Not only the Earth, but the entire Solar system, and as much of the universe as he can reach under the laws of nature, are man's rightful field of activity.

3. By expanding throughout the universe, man fulfills his destiny as an element of life, endowed with the power of reason and the wisdom of the moral law within himself.

The Love of the Other

The subsuming process of all these works—and what lies at the heart of LaRouche's proposal—is mankind's discovery of the meaning of mankind. What is the purpose for which we exist? How do we implement and advance the creative power which is uniquely human? LaRouche developed his four laws from a Hamiltonian standard based on an underlying principle of an unconditional—that is, agapic—love for mankind, to create its future.

The Hamiltonian principles which set the standards for our nation's economic policies do not arise from the standpoint of money having some intrinsic value, but from an understanding of the value of the human mind and of increasing the productive powers of mind. Hamilton's principles of economics come from the idea of happiness, an agapic principle adopted in our Declaration of Independence from the German philosopher and economist Gottfried Leibniz. That is what you will find when you read the four major reports to the Congress by Alexander Hamilton.

This is the essence of what the British Empire and its financial oligarchy—represented by Wall Street and its stooges—have made every effort to destroy since the murder of Hamilton by the British tool Aaron Burr. Our nation's greatest leaders—including John Quincy Adams, Abraham Lincoln, Franklin Roosevelt, and John F. Kennedy—understood and consciously engaged in this fight to defeat this enemy of the creative progress of mankind.

These Presidents understood more than just Hamilton's conception of national credit or of banking. They understood a unique principle of the United States to be the advance of the productive and creative powers of every living being in this nation and on this planet—what LaRouche would later define in his science of physical economy as the increase in relative potential population density.

Only Yesterday

President Franklin Roosevelt, a devout student of Alexander Hamilton, was inspired by his great-grandfather, Isaac Roosevelt, who worked directly with Hamilton. This laid the basis for FDR's victory over the Wall Street looters of his day and his ability to unleash the greatest productive machine the world had ever seen. The period of Franklin Roosevelt through that of John F. Kennedy was known as the Golden Age of Productivity. Today we need a golden age of productivity for the world, and that is just the future that China has set out to create, with more than half of the world already joining in. The United States must take its rightful place and make its due contribution in bringing about this very future.

Our Golden Age of Productivity continued with the development of our space program under the visionary leadership of great space pioneers such as the little known genius, the German-American aeronautical engineer, Krafft Ehricke.

When the National Aeronautics and Space Act was passed by Congress in 1958, creating NASA, the declaration of purpose stated: "The Congress hereby declares that it is the policy of the United States that activities in space should be devoted to peaceful purposes for the benefit of all mankind." The Act goes on to define that the aeronautical and space activities of the United States shall be so conducted as to contribute materially to one or more of the following objectives:

We must have a Fusion-Driver Crash Program. Shown here, the test-bed of South Korea's superconducting tokamak fusion reactor, KSTAR.

1. The expansion of human knowledge of phenomena in the atmosphere and space.

2. The improvement of the usefulness, performance, speed, safety, and efficiency of aeronautical and space vehicles.

3. The development and operation of vehicles capable of carrying instruments, equipment, supplies, and living organisms through space.

4. The establishment of long-range studies of the potential benefits to be gained from, the opportunities for, and the problems involved in the utilization of aeronautical and space activities for peaceful and scientific purposes.

5. The preservation of the role of the United States as a leader in aeronautical and space science and technology and in the application thereof to the conduct of peaceful activities within and outside the atmosphere.

6. The making available to agencies directly concerned with national defenses of discoveries that have military value or significance, and the furnishing by such agencies, to the civilian agency established to direct and control non-

military aeronautical and space activities, of information as to discoveries which have value or significance to that agency.

7. Cooperation by the United States with other nations and groups of nations in work done pursuant to this Act and in the peaceful application of the results, thereof.

8. The most effective utilization of the scientific and engineering resources of the United States, with close cooperation among all interested agencies of the United States in order to avoid unnecessary duplication of effort, facilities, and equipment.

Devotion to the exploration of space must start with a love for, and commitment to the creative development of all mankind. The vision for space exploration and settlement was never merely a race or a matter of military dominance, contrary to the wild ideas of some in the scientific community. The space program as envisioned by Ehricke was a commitment to the future of mankind. When NASA was established, Ehricke had already written some profound works on the idea of space travel and what he called mankind's extraterrestrial imperative. He had written an imaginary account of space travel in the year 2050, in 1948—ten years before NASA (published in part in *21st Century Science & Technology*, Spring 2003).

Ehricke understood the unique quality of mankind

that defies the oligarchy's rejection of our creative human identity—that creative identity which is essential for mankind's mission to develop our Universe. He states, "By expanding through the Universe, man fulfills his destiny as an element of life; endowed with the power of reason and the wisdom of the moral law within himself."

President Kennedy's thinking intersected Ehricke's concept of mankind. At the groundbreaking ceremony for the Hanford nuclear generating plant in Hanford, Washington, on September 26, 1963, he said, "This great, rich country of ours has a long, unfinished agenda, but it has always had that agenda in creative times, and this is a creative time in our country and throughout the world."

The Path to Fusion Power

LaRouche's fourth law calls for a Fusion-Driver Crash Program. Obama's rejection of the "essential distinction of man from all lower forms of life" was precisely the idea at the core of his attack on our nation's space program and his rejection of a revolution in science through a fusion driver program. His attacks on our nation's manned space program and our fusion research programs have been brutal. Obama had the nerve to say that we don't need any "fancy fusion." Now you've seen not only the shutdown of our manned space program, but the termination of work toward breakthroughs in advanced scientific and technical programs, such as the fusion research and development programs at MIT, with serious repercussions for the fusion program at Princeton. And you have seen the U.S. rejection of cooperation with other nations on such projects.

It is all being shut down because we didn't demand Glass-Steagall. We didn't insist on the Hamiltonian credit system to put the necessary credit into these great scientific endeavors and large-scale infrastructure. We chose instead to bail out Wall Street, to protect the looters and let more and more people die. This was not the standard of Hamilton, nor of Franklin Roosevelt or John F. Kennedy.

Kennedy understood the importance of the nation's space program as a science driver program for progress in the economy across a broad front. And he understood nuclear power production as the complement to the space program, in terms of its effects on the economy as a whole. At the Hanford groundbreaking ceremony, he said, "We must hasten the development of low-cost atomic power. I think we should lead the world in this.... Our experts estimate that half of all electric energy generated in the United States will come from nuclear sources."

Kennedy knew that it was essential to unleash the creative powers of every person in this nation. At Hanford, he spoke of "All of the trained and educated men and women who are making our country over, who are building a better standard of living for our people—this is a time when we wish to encourage the release of energy, human energy, which is the most extraordinary of all." Today that vision for human development and cooperation is being carried out by what China is doing in the development of its space and nuclear programs.

Implement LaRouche's Four Laws!

LaRouche is emphatic that China has to be a model from the standpoint of the space program. The standard that China has set for itself and the world reflects nothing less than a renaissance and a new paradigm for the progress of all mankind. China's space program is organized around a national commitment to cultural and scientific advance, and because of this, China is now going to the far side of the Moon, unlike any other nation—doing something that no other nation has done. What does this mean? This is a breakthrough toward a revolution in science, a breakthrough for the benefit and progress of all mankind. This is the very principle of LaRouche's four laws.

What China represents for the world today is what the United States and its founding principles once represented. What is required of our nation today is the revolution in science that LaRouche is calling for—a revolution in the conception of the nature of mankind: what it means to be human, what we are as a species.

We have to pull our nation out of the depths of the dark age conditions that have dominated much of the trans-Atlantic world in the recent decades. We must stop the mass killings and reverse the upward trend in suicides in the United States and around the world. That is why we are going to implement LaRouche's four laws now. It is time to shut down Wall Street now! End the financial speculation! We must redefine our national commitment to humanity. We have the potential to bring about a Renaissance for all of mankind, if we choose to do so—based on a true understanding of what mankind is, and what our future must be. It is time to begin the implementation of LaRouche's four laws by re-instituting the Glass-Steagall Act. Demand that Congress get back to Washington now, to pass Glass-Steagall! It has a responsibility to this nation and to mankind.

Philippines to Obama: Keep Your Aid!

by Michael Billington

The tremendous transformation to optimism and moral strength taking place within the Philippines, under the leadership of President Rodrigo Duterte, is captured in the following brief report, reprinted from the EIR *Daily Alert Service. The hysterical diatribe against Duterte coming from Obama and his ilk over Duterte's War on Drugs is not surprising, given that Obama is pushing drug legalization across the country and around the world, contributing to the worst drug epidemic in American history and tearing every community in the country apart.*

Some of the Cabinet officials referenced here have been technocrats in the past, serving Philippine governments subservient to the Washington and London bankers, but have gained courage and moral fortitude from Duterte's leadership. Duterte has dedicated himself to ending the hunger, poverty, and drug addiction of his country, and to totally rejecting Obama's effort to use his country as a battle station for a war on China.

—Michael Billington

King Rodriguez - Presidential Communications Operation Office

President Rodrigo Duterte presents a chart illustrating a drug trade network of high-level drug syndicates in the Philippines during a press conference, July 7, 2016.

Oct. 7—"Go to Hell with your aid!" Was this Philippine President Duterte again telling the U.S. that the people of the Philippines were no longer America's Little Brown Brothers? Close—but in fact it is a quote from President Sukarno of Indonesia in 1964, after the assassination of JFK (who had supported Sukarno) and the launching of a "regime change" operation against him from London and Washington, as part of America's tragic turn to British imperialism and colonial wars.

But Duterte said essentially the same thing yesterday: "Go away, bring your money to somewhere else. We will survive as a nation." Speaking to police officers in the southern city of Butuan, Duterte said, "How do you look at us, [as] mendicants? We will survive. Even if we'll go through hardships, we will survive. But we will never, never compromise our dignity. If you think it is high time for you guys to withdraw your assistance, go ahead, we will not beg for it."

An End to Subservience Declared

And not only the President is standing up to Obama:

• Foreign Secretary Perfecto Yasay posted on his website a statement titled, "America has failed us." It reads, in part: "Breaking away from the shackling dependency of the Philippines to effectively address both internal and external security threats has become imperative in putting an end to our nation's subservience to United States interests." He said that, despite being granted independence in 1946, "the former colonial masters held onto invisible chains that reined us in toward dependency and submission as little brown

CC/Mike Gonzalez

Philippines' alliance with the United States is at a dead end in favor of infrastructure investment discussions with Asian nations, to fight crushing poverty.

brothers not capable of true independence and freedom." He said that the "carrot and stick" policy had been "effectively used all through the long years since our independence to force Filipinos into submission to American demands and interests. This is what [President Duterte] is now trying to liberate us from."

• General (ret.) Delfin Lorenzana, the Defense Secretary, speaking to the foreign press today, was asked about Duterte's charge that the CIA was out to assassinate him. He said that he had asked U.S. Ambassador Philip Goldberg about it, who said, "We don't do that." It is not known whether Lorenzana reminded the Ambassador of Obama's weekly drone kill list. Lorenzana did note, however, that President Duterte "keeps saying to us in private, 'I don't think I can solve this problem during my time,'" asking them to continue the mission if he were to be assassinated. Lorenzana said Duterte was "not fatalistic," but was aware that "a person's life is very fleeting."

Lorenzana said his country had faced similar attacks from the U.S. during the time of Marcos, concluding: "Personally, I welcome this development. It's time maybe to reassess our relationship. Maybe we should reassess what we should be getting from the alliance . . .

It's part of maybe growing up. We should not be too dependent on one country," adding that he was looking to China and Russia for possible arms purchases and other help.

• In Washington, D.C., the Philippine Secretaries of Finance, Budget, and Socioeconomic Planning spoke at the Philippine Embassy Wednesday, and all three were extremely optimistic about Duterte's commitment to reversing the economic disaster left over from the past administrations, openly admitting that the poverty rate in the country is the worst in the Association of Southeast Asian Nations (ASEAN), that the wealth gap is horrendous, that the "oligarchy" living in Manila had ignored any development outside of the capital (although the infrastructure in Manila is also disastrous), and that agricultural output and farmer income is literally declining from an already low base.

Threats Rejected

When an American "wealth management" financier rose to warn them that "Duterte's statements and behavior" were causing her clients to pull out of the Philippines and that they had better stop him, Finance Secretary Carlos Dominguez responded that he had been meeting with Canadians, Japanese, and others who were very anxious to invest in the country, and that the government would be meeting with China this month to discuss infrastructure investments. "If some of you in the U.S. are having second thoughts about investing," he said, "it is too bad for you to miss out, but we have plenty of investors."

This is a powerful model for the world's developing nations of the necessary fight against Obama's imperial warmongering and economic looting. Projected U.S. aid to the Philippines for 2017 is a paltry $188 million and perhaps a few worn out Coast Guard vessels. The United States long ago stopped building any infrastructure in the Philippines, or anywhere else for that matter.

Obama and the Third Offset: From Strategic Bluff to War of Annihilation

by Carl Osgood

Oct. 10—President Barack Obama is a killer, but he's also a faker. "Obama and company are trying to intimidate the world into submission — but it's not likely to work. There are many nations and forces in Asia and even in Europe who can't be convinced by this." That was *EIR* Editor-in-Chief Lyndon LaRouche's judgment in discussion on Oct. 6 of the strong Russian Defense Ministry warnings against any U.S. attack on Syrian and Russian forces in Syria, and the furious threat to "beat Russia down," delivered by U.S. Army Chief of Staff Gen. Mark Milley in a Washington, D.C., speech Oct. 4. Milley's outburst coincided with a "leak" to Josh Rogin of the *Washington Post* that active options for U.S. attacks on Syrian (and inevitably Russian) armed forces are under discussion in the White House.

LaRouche added that "Obama would like to say that Russia is his number-one enemy, but his threats are not true. General war is beyond anything Obama can understand. He'd like to have almighty power, but he doesn't have it any more. He's more like just a British royal family agent with a bad smell." Nonetheless in drone killings, in Libya, in Iraq, in Syria, now in Yemen, etc., Obama is a "lying mass murderer," LaRouche concluded. "When you say those three words —'lying mass murderer'— you've got him."

Old Wine in New Bottles

The murders by drone, which Obama orders every Tuesday, are an uglier caricature of the "air power" doctrine than, for instance, H.G. Wells' seminal "Shape of Things to Come" of 1933. Death is dealt out from the air by omniscient supermen against whom there is neither defense nor retaliation.

After World War II, American enthusiasts for the 1945 firebombing of Dresden and for "systems analy-

White House/Pete Souza

LaRouche: "Obama and company are trying to intimidate the world, but it's not likely to work." Here, President Obama with members of his national security team in the Situation Room of the White House.

U.S. Army Chief of Staff Gen. Mark Milley proposed to "beat Russia down" in a Washington speech Oct. 4. Here he testifies before the Senate Appropriations Committee, Feb. 24, 2016.

Deputy Secretary of Defense Robert Work, the chief proponent of the third offset strategy, which Work sees as an updated version of Blitzkrieg.

sis," formed the RAND Corporation to advise the Air Force. Now Obama's proclivities have caused him to embrace an incompetent strain of RAND Corporation thinking that has been resident at the Pentagon since at least 1973. This is signified today in the Pentagon's so-called "Third Offset Strategy," which is intended—or so its proponents say—to lead to technological innovations that will help the U.S. military overcome advantages that, in particular, Russia and China have gained in the past decade and a half in developing their military services.

The chief proponent of the third offset strategy is Deputy Secretary of Defense Robert Work, who told *Breaking Defense*'s Sydney Freedberg in an interview last February, that the third offset is "about human-machine collaborative combat networks." In other words, Freedberg wrote, Work wants artificial intelligence to help humans make decisions, computers to keep "an unblinking eye," to sort through gigabytes of "big data" for actionable intelligence and detect "subtle patterns" in the behavior of adversaries, and to execute military actions that are too fast for human reflexes.

The term "third offset," itself refers to what its proponents have defined as the first two offsets: President

Eisenhower's "New Look" nuclear doctrine of the 1950s, and the DoD's technological push in the 1970s that resulted in stealth, precision-guided weapons, and other technologies that came to fruition beginning in the late 1980s. "The whole vision of the offset is to make the human better, not to make the machines better," Work told Freedberg. "We're building on the [existing] battle networks that employ conventional weapons, and we're vastly improving them by utilizing [artificial intelligence] and autonomy ... to allow humans to make better decisions, to perform better in combat, and to be more effective."

If this sounds at all familiar, that's because it's really old (synthetic) wine in a new bottle. It's a new generation of the "Revolution in Military Affairs" (RMA) that failed so spectacularly in the sands of Iraq and the poppy fields of Afghanistan. The RMA originated in the Pentagon's "Office of Net Assessment," headed from 1973 until last year by Andrew Marshall, who began his career in 1949 "thinking about the unthinkable," that is, how to fight nuclear war. While Marshall was thinking about fighting nuclear wars against the Soviet Union and China, he was also engaged in building a network of disciples throughout the military and the national security think-tank community, from the 1970s on, who would then embed his method of thinking into the relevant institutions.

The key think-tank in Marshall's network is the "Center for Strategic and Budgetary Assessments" (CSBA), founded by retired Army Col. Andrew Krepinevich, a 1989-1990 alumnus of Marshall's office. The CSBA gave us the "Air-Sea Battle" operational concept in 2010, for waging war against China in the South China Sea. The "third offset" strategy, which the CSBA introduced with a 94-page report in late 2014, builds on the earlier work of the

U.S. Army (ret.) Col. Andrew Krepinevich, a member of Andrew Marshall's network who founded the Center for Strategic and Budgetary Assessments. It employs Marshall's outlook and methods. In 2010 it produced the Air-Sea Battle operational concept for war against China in the South China Sea.

U.S. Army/Mr. Scott Davis

The "third offset strategy," like the earlier versions of the so-called Revolution in Military Affairs, comes from the Pentagon's Office of Net Assessment, long headed by Andrew Marshall. Marshall, shown here, began his career in 1949 with Herman Kahn, planning how to fight nuclear war against the Soviet Union and China.

RMA and the Air-Sea Battle concept. Robert Work spent the George W. Bush years working at CSBA, where he was well indoctrinated in the method of thinking of Andrew Marshall, if he wasn't already familiar with it before then. He was appointed Undersecretary of the Navy in 2009. Work moved to his present job in 2013, and was put in charge of the "third offset" effort by then-Secretary of Defense Chuck Hagel.

That the third offset is derived from the RMA is not lost on journalist Freedberg, cited above, who reports that both deal with the combination of precision-guided weapons, long range surveillance, and the networks required to get targeting information from the sensor to the shooter.

However, Freedberg claims they come from opposite directions. The RMA came out of the 1991 Gulf War, which convinced strategists that the American combination of precision, surveillance, and networks would always give America an unmatchable advantage in future conflicts. The third offset, on the other hand "arises from the unhappy realization that the Russian

bear is back, China is rising, and they're rapidly fielding the very combination of precision, surveillance, and networks that was once a U.S. monopoly," Freedberg writes. "Worse, they're developing tactics and technologies, especially in cyberspace and the radio spectrum, specifically to baffle, blind, or destroy our networked war-machine. If our adversaries are learning how to copy and counter our current advantages, we need to offset their growing power—hence the name—by finding new advantages."

The automatic assumption that China and Russia are U.S. adversaries is but one carryover from Andrew Marshall's thinking. During the Cold War, Marshall had focused all of his attention on the Soviet Union, but when the Soviet Union collapsed, he turned to China, commissioning translations of many Chinese military writings, in much the same way that he had earlier approached the Soviet Union.

One result of the focus on China was a study called "Asia 2025," which came out in early 2000. According to a *Washington Post* article at the time, the report pos-

Exercise Valiant Shield 2016 tested the Air-Sea Battle operational concept in the Philippine Sea.

tulated that China will be a future threat to the United States whether it is strong or weak. This was the thinking that continued through the Air-Sea Battle concept—though the Pentagon tried hard to play it down—and is fully embedded in the third offset strategy. This also happens to be fully coherent with President Obama's "Asia Pivot," announced in January 2012, by which the United States would shift the majority of its military forces to the Western Pacific to counter a "rising China."

The *Blitzkrieg* Outlook

Another sign that the third offset isn't really all that different from the RMA, is the attachment to the Nazi Blitzkrieg model of operations of 1939-1940. According to Mark Pomerleau, writing in the Sept. 19, 2016 issue of the *C4ISR Journal,* Robert Work has described the end goal the third offset seeks to achieve, through the lens of the interwar period of the 1920s and 1930s. All nations had access to the same technologies, such

as radios, airplanes and tanks, "but only the Germans put everything together into an operational concept called *Blitzkrieg,*" Work said. "Now we were all fast followers. As soon as we saw it, we all said: 'God, why didn't we think of that?' By 1944 we were 'out-blitzkrieging' the Germans."

This is remarkably similar to the language used in an article by Sen. Dan Coats (R-Ind.) that appeared in the *Joint Force Quarterly* in 1999. Coats was one of the architects of what became the U.S. Joint Forces Command's "Joint Experimentation Directorate," where many of the RMA concepts were developed into operational doctrine during the G.W. Bush years.

Coats wrote that only by integrating information age technology "with changes in organization and doctrine, based on truly joint concepts, can our capabilities be maximized. It was this type of integration that made *Blitzkrieg* and carrier aviation [into] revolutionary new technology used in new ways with new force structures." He added that "During the 1930s, combat aircraft, tanks, and radio communications were available in both France and Germany. But through the efforts of von Seekt and Guderian, the Germans leveraged them with new organizations and doctrine to develop more effective war-fighting capabilities. Thus, the development of the *Blitzkrieg* offers insight into creating change."

What Work is ignoring and Coats before him, is that the *Blitzkrieg* model of operations failed when it came up against an enemy—the Soviet Union— that was able to muster both the will and the capacity to resist it.

Sen. Dan Coats (R-Ind.), writing in Joint Force Quarterly *in 1999: "The development of* Blitzkrieg *in the 1930s through the efforts of von Seekt and Guderian "offers insight into creating change."*

Why the RMA Failed

In earlier times, the proponents of failed ideas might have been fired from any positions of responsibility and consequently faded from history. In post-Cold War Washington, D.C., they get to change the names of their failed ideas and do the same thing all over again. The Revolution in Military Affairs failed because its thinkers didn't take into account the human factor in warfare,— or better said, their whole *raison d'etre* is precisely to oppose the human factor.

The RMA was encapsulated in buzz-phrases like "effects-based operations (EBO)," "rapid decisive operations," "operational net assessment," "standing joint-force headquarters," and so forth, that were flying around the halls of the Pentagon and military think-tanks in 2001 and 2002. As was explained to this author in 2002, the hypothesis behind all this was that a standing joint force headquarters that uses "operational net assessment" and employs "effects-based operations," can achieve "decision superiority," enabling "rapid decisive operations."

As most informed people are aware by now, the invasion and occupation of Iraq, beginning in March 2003, went nothing like that. It was neither rapid nor decisive, and bogged down quickly into irregular war-

fare. The U.S. Army and the U.S. Marine Corps were forced to abandon the buzz-phrases and learn how to fight a counterinsurgency campaign instead, exactly the opposite of what the RMA had predicted.

The RMA also failed in Israel. One study, produced by the U.S. Army's Combat Studies Institute, attributed the failure of the Israeli military campaign in Lebanon in 2006 to precisely the operational concepts of the RMA. They were not designed to inflict actual military defeat on Hezbollah. Rather they were supposed to produce "effects" that would force Hezbollah out of southern Lebanon and cause it to disarm.

The IDF began with an air campaign that was supposed to produce those effects, and when that failed, the Israeli army launched a ground campaign that was supposed to do the same thing. Instead, it ran into an expertly prepared conventional but decentralized defense that was entirely unperturbed by Israeli efforts to generate "effects." It was able to inflict heavy casualties on poorly prepared Israeli ground forces, whose major experience over the previous several years had been in occupation duty in the Palestinian territories. Ultimately, the RMA was about "behavior modification" of the enemy, not the proven principles of military campaigning.

The concepts of the RMA were finally demolished by Gen. James Mattis, now retired, but who was then commander of the U.S. Joint Forces Command. In an August 2008 memo, he cited the Israeli experience in Lebanon as well as the U.S. war in Iraq. Mattis noted that these concepts "have not delivered on their advertised benefits," and that "a clear understanding of these concepts has proven problematic and elusive for U.S. and multinational personnel." Among the conclusions that the Army, the Marine Corps, and other observers have come to, Mattis wrote, were the following:

CC/IraqVet225

A U.S. armored vehicle, put out of action by an improvised explosive device (IED), in Iraq. According to the doctrine of the Revolution in Military Affairs, determined civilian resistance was expected to be insignificant. It wasn't.

• EBO assumes an unachievable level of predictability.

• It cannot correctly anticipate reactions of complex systems.

• It discounts the human dimension of war (passion, imagination, will power, and unpredictability, among other human characteristics).

The third offset is moving in the same sort of direction as the RMA did but, according to its critics, is even less developed conceptually than the RMA. "The Third Offset Strategy resembles a high tech version of the casting call for the tryouts for *America's Got Talent*; even the producers have no idea who will show up or how they will perform," wrote the Lexington Institute's Dan Gouré in a June 14, 2016 article in *The National Interest*.

Gouré is convinced that the third offset is nothing more than a smokescreen to cover the fact that the Obama Administration is shrinking the U.S. military, both in size and capability. "The hope is that the Third Offset Strategy will do for the military what is already being done for parking garages, fast food restaurants and retail stores: reduce the need for human beings." There is certainly room for such improvements in the military, Gouré went on, but there are practical limits to how far that can be taken.

"The bigger danger is that Department of Defense will become enamored of its 'new offset' strategy and cut current programs and forces in anticipation of great results emerging from its investments in automation, big data, and robots," he concludes. "There is a long history of the Pentagon and the White House promising huge leaps forward in military capabilities for future systems that are just Power-Point slides, but cutting real capabilities now."

The problem is that war is never quite as easy as the RMA proponents think they can make it. "A lot of times when the Army talks about the future of war, we don't have a super-happy message," said Lt. Gen. H.R. McMaster, deputy commander of the U.S. Army Training and Doctrine Command and long a harsh critic of utopian ideas about warfighting, according to a Nov. 14, 2014 article in *Foreign Policy* on the debate over strategy in Iraq and Syria. "We're saying: 'War is hard. War is difficult to resolve.' But there are those who actually have a happier message, but the problem is, it's self-delusion. It's visions of future war that are fundamentally flawed." It is with that sort of delusion that President Obama is taking us into confrontation with Russia and China, a confrontation in which he cannot control the outcome despite the delusions of the RMA crowd. This is why Lyndon LaRouche characterizes his actions as a bluff.

In modern war since Ulysses S. Grant, or "total war," the "human factors" of passionate moral commitment, total dedication, and creativity,—the same ones that Gen. Mattis cited—are ultimately decisive. Forget the childish "offset" theories as such. In Andy Marshall, Robert Work, Gen. Milley and their like, there is a passionate commitment to deny—to annul—the human factor. What they have done with their power in the past, and what they are doing with Obama now, should demonstrate that this is no different from Obama's passionate commitment to mass murder.

GLOBAL FINANCIAL CRASH AND DANGER OF WAR!

Is It One Minute Past Midnight?

By Helga Zepp-LaRouche, chair of the German political party Civil Rights Movement Solidarity (BüSo)

Oct. 7—A perfect storm is brewing: The Damocles sword of an imminent collapse of the trans-Atlantic financial system is hanging over the world, while the closely related strategic confrontation between the United States and Russia could shift at any moment from the now ongoing Cold War into a direct military confrontation—potentially the end of mankind. There is a way out, but it requires dumping geopolitics immediately, and thinking in terms of a completely new paradigm.

"How hot will the new Cold War be?" was the headline of *Bild-Zeitung* Oct. 7. The German government's special coordinator for Russian policy , Gernot Erler, no longer rules out a direct military confrontation between the United States and Russia; Wolfgang Ischinger, head of the Munich Security Conference, considers this danger to be "significant." Security experts Steven Simon and Jonathan Stevenson in the *New York Times* of Oct. 6, warn: "But the truth is that it is too late for the United States to wade deeper into the Syrian conflict without risking a major war."

This danger is absolutely real, but the way the acute war danger is presented in most Western media can only be deemed pre-war propaganda, which demonizes the prospective war opponent—in this case, Russian President Vladimir Putin. The suffering of the Syrian population is intolerable, but the chronology of events leading to it has been suppressed. Who is responsible for the policy of regime change? Who has played the "Islamic card" against the Soviet Union since 1975 and built up the constantly renamed grouplets—from the Mujaheddin to Al-Qaeda, Al-Nusra, ISIS, and others—and supplied them with weapons up to the present day, as journalist Jürgen Todenhöfer, among others, has stressed in recent interviews?

Who has covered up the true circumstances behind the September 11th attacks? Who has launched the wars against Afghanistan, Iraq, Libya, and Syria on the basis of well-known lies? Who turns a blind eye to Saudi Arabia's barbaric war in Yemen?

'Deep Emotional Breakdown'

Secretary of State John Kerry and Russian Foreign Minister Sergei Lavrov had just negotiated a ceasefire in Syria when the U.S. Air Force "by mistake" bombed positions of the Syrian army which had been known for months, killing 60 soldiers and wounding one hundred—only to then blame Russian forces for the attack on the UN aid convoy in Aleppo, while providing no evidence whatsoever. The Russian government hence concluded that the Obama Administration was out to

wikipedia

Free Syrian Army soldiers cleaning their rifles in Aleppo. Like Al-Qaeda, Al-Nusra, and ISIS, the Free Syrian Army is a surrogate for the regime-change powers.

sabotage Kerry's strategy. It suspended the treaty for the disposal of weapons-grade plutonium with the United States, and announced the deployment of S-300 and S-400 anti-missile defense systems to Syria. Given this situation, demands for the establishment of no-fly zones and so-called safe zones along the Turkish border with Syria—which could only be enforced by military means—are a direct declaration of intent to confront Russia.

The spokesman for the Russian Defense Ministry, Igor Konaschenko, warned all those who were toying with the idea of direct military operations against the Syrian army that the S-300 and S-400 anti-missile defense systems had surprises in store for them, and warned against the illusion of being able to deploy stealth bombers. Russian Deputy Foreign Minister Sergei Ryabkov commented on Washington's announcement that it was abandoning any cooperation on a Syrian diplomatic settlement, that the decision makers in the United States are letting themselves be guided by emotion, rather than cool calculation. He said: "They are making every decision against the backdrop of a deep emotional breakdown."

State Department Photo

Secretary Kerry and Russian Foreign Minister Lavrov speak to the press before a bilateral meeting in Geneva, Sept. 9, 2016.

The Banking Absurdity

One can also assume in good conscience that the decision makers in the United States are not being guided behind the scenes by cool calculation in the case of the trans-Atlantic financial system. Because if they were, they would admit the total bankruptcy of the neo-liberal monetarist system and carry out an immediate reorganization on the basis of a global Glass-Steagall/bank separation system. Instead, the IMF and the World Bank at their semi-annual Oct. 7-9 meeting in Washington sought to continue their bankrupt policy, and made the incredible argument that the rise of populist protest movements against their policies was responsible for the crisis. That was just as absurd as their demand that China and India restrict their issuance of credit. The IMF criticized precisely those two nations that are the motors of growth in the world economy!

In private discussions among several participants in these meetings, the participants were horrified to realize that the entire European and American banking system is not only hopelessly bankrupt, but that its

criminal character has led to what is deadly for the financial sector—namely, a full-scale crisis of confidence. The unspoken problem was and remains Deutsche Bank, with its derivatives risk of 42 trillion euros—a sum about 12 times the annual Gross Domestic Product of the entire German economy! And all the banks which are allegedly too big to fail, are counterparties in Deutsche Bank's derivatives contracts, and can sink together with it.

The *New York Times* lamented Oct. 6 that Deutsche Bank could turn out to be the new Lehman Brothers, and quoted Harvard Professor Hal Scott, who said he hoped "there's a global game plan because that's what it would take. If Deutsche Bank sets off contagion, it would start in Europe. Who would be next? This would require global coordination."

The Only Workable Solution

To avoid the meltdown of the trans-Atlantic financial system—looming in October or November, at the latest—which would lead to chaos worldwide and bring the war danger to a boiling point, there is only one workable solution: the immediate, internationally coordinated implementation of the Four Laws that Lyndon LaRouche proposed on June 18, 2014:

1. The immediate re-establishment of the Glass-Steagall bank separation system, exactly as Franklin D. Roosevelt established it in 1933. In practice, this would mean the cancellation of the vast majority of unpayable debts and outstanding derivatives contracts.

1
Glass-Steagall Bank Separation

Franklin D. Roosevelt signs Glass-Steagall Act, 1933.
National Archives

2
National Banking Credit Creation

First National Bank of the United States, Philadelphia.
Library of Congress

3
International Credit System

Chinese-funded railway construction in Kenya.
beyase.com

4
Science Driver

An artist's rendition of China's planned space station.
China.org

2. Every country must introduce national banking in the tradition of Alexander Hamilton, which will replace the current policy of credit creation—by independent central banks for the benefit of gamblers—with the model used by Hamilton, Lincoln, and FDR, as well as by the postwar *Kreditanstalt für Wiederaufbau* (Bank for Reconstruction) in Germany.

3. An international credit system must be created, tasked with raising the productivity of the real economy and the living standards of the populations of all nations, which can be done by promoting scientific and technological progress, and a real rise in the energy-flux density of the production process.

4. We need a science driver for the economy, namely a crash program for harnessing fusion energy and using fusion energy technology, and international cooperation on space research.

It is not surprising that the impulse for such a reorganization is not coming from the United States or Europe. The closest approximation to LaRouche's proposals was presented by China at the recent G-20 Summit in Hangzhou, where that nation proposed a new global financial architecture and the reform of the world economy on the basis of innovation and growth. It is to be expected that these proposals will translate into new initiatives at the annual conference of the BRICS nations, this year in Goa, India in mid-October. The importance of the banks that China and the BRICS nations have created—such as the Asian International Infrastructure Bank, the New Development Bank, the Silk Road and Maritime Silk Road Funds, as well as the Contingency Reserve Arrangement—will grow.

Glass-Steagall Is the Next Step

As for the United States, Lyndon LaRouche has called for the U.S. Congress to immediately leave off election campaigning and return to Washington to adopt Glass-Steagall legislation. Given the tremendous opposition from Wall Street, that won't be an easy task, but the power of Wall Street has shrunk enormously because of the anger of the population over the criminal character of many of these banks that are going bankrupt, due not least to the growing financial fines for their frauds. The sale of toxic paper to credulous clients, the LIBOR manipulation, the million-fold creation of fictitious accounts, accounting fraud, money-laundering, and on and on—the list of crimes is enormous.

The broad mobilization in the United States by the LaRouche movement and relatives of the victims of 9/11, the first responders, firemen, and of other institutions led to the game-changing vote in Congress to override President Obama's veto of the Justice Against Sponsors of Terrorism Act (JASTA). Now more than 200 organizations are building on this success, making the stance of Congressmen and Senators on Glass-Steagall the criterion for their re-election in November and confronting them with their responsibility as they campaign for re-election.

In Europe too, we must force the parliaments—through a broad-based mobilization of the population—to end the casino economy with the immediate adoption of Glass-Steagall banking separation laws, in order to reshape economic policy according to LaRouche's Four Laws, and to rebuild—together with China, Russia, and hopefully a United States reorganized under Glass-Steagall—the countries that have been destroyed by senseless, barbaric wars. The development of the New Silk Road in the Middle East and Africa is not only the sole humane solution to the refugee crisis, but also a test of Europe's moral fitness to survive.

The war danger can only be overcome if we replace geopolitical confrontation with a totally new paradigm of international collaboration for the common aims of Mankind.

Every Day Counts In Today's Showdown To Save Civilization

That's why you need EIR's **Daily Alert Service**, a strategic overview compiled with the input of Lyndon LaRouche, and delivered to your email 5 days a week.

For example: On Jan. 7, EIR's Daily Alert featured the British hand behind the pattern of global provocations toward war. Of special note is British Intelligence's role in instigating the Saudi Kingdom's attempt to set off a Sunni-Shia war. This religious war has been the intent of British strategy since the Blair-Bush attack on Iraq in 2003.

We also uniquely update you regularly on the progress toward the release of the suppressed 28 pages of the Congressional Inquiry on 9/11, which would expose the Saudi role.

Every edition highlights the reality of the impending financial crash/bail-in policies that would realize the British goal of mass depopulation.

This is intelligence you need to act on, if we are going to survive as a nation and a species. Can you really afford to be without it?

THURSDAY, JANUARY 7, 2016

Volume 2, Number 97

EIR Daily Alert Service

P.O. Box 17390, Washington, DC 20041-0390

- British Crown Pushing War and Genocide in 2016
- Financial Mudslide Goes On; Monetarist Tyranny Gloats over Bail-Ins
- Moody's Downgrades Portugal's Novo Banco
- Puerto Rico's Default: It's Every Vulture for Himself
- Wide Glass-Steagall Debate Set Off Again by Sanders Speech
- MI6 Mouthpiece Evans-Pritchard Touts Persian Gulf Chaos
- North Korea Tests a Miniaturized Hydrogen Bomb
- Uighur Terrorists Found in Indonesia
- Foreign Investors Are Flocking In to China

EDITORIAL

British Crown Pushing War and Genocide in 2016

www.ingramcontent.com/pod-product-compliance
Lightning Source LLC
Chambersburg PA
CBHW051953280526
45789CB00009B/3272